Dinner

Moira Buffini studied English/Drama at Goldsmiths'
College and trained as an actor at the Welsh College of
Music and Drama. She acted professionally for five years,
winning the *Time Out* Award for her performance in
Jordan. Whilst a drama teacher in Holloway Prison, she
directed two productions, *Two* by Jim Cartwright and
Jean-Paul Sartre's adaptation of *The Trojan Women*.
Writing for theatre includes *Loveplay* (2001) for the RSC
at the Pit; *The Games Room* (2000) at Soho Theatre;
Silence (1999), commissioned by the National Theatre
Studio, performed at the Birmingham Rep and Plymouth
Theatre Royal, and winner of the Susan Smith Blackburn
prize; *Gabriel* (1997), for the Machine Room; and
Jordan, co-written with Anne Reynolds, at the Lilian
Baylis/BAC/Gate and winner of the Writers' Guild Award
for Best Fringe Play. Her first screenplay, *Northern Soul*,
is currently in development.

MOIRA BUFFINI

Dinner

faber and faber

First published in 2002
by Faber and Faber Limited
3 Queen Square, London WC1N 3AU

Typeset by Country Setting, Kingsdown, Kent CT14 8ES
Printed in England by Mackays of Chatham plc, Chatham, Kent

A CIP record for this book
is available from the British Library

ISBN 0–571–21851–2

2 4 6 8 10 9 7 5 3

To my sisters
Fiona and Nuala

Dinner was first performed in the Loft at the National Theatre on 18 October 2002. The cast, in order of speaking, was as follows:

Paige Harriet Walter
Lars Nicholas Farrell
Wynne Penny Downie
Hal Adrian Rawlins
Siân Catherine McCormack
Mike Paul Rattray
The Waiter Christopher Ettridge

Director Fiona Buffini
Designer Rachel Blues
Lighting Designer Pete Bull
Sound Designer Rich Walsh
Company Voice Work Kate Godfrey

This production of **Dinner** was revived at Wydham's Theatre, London, on 9 December 2003, with the following cast changes: Adrian Lukis as Hal, Flora Montgomery as Siân, Paul Kaye as Mike, and Paul Sirr as The Waiter.

Characters

THE DINERS

Paiges

Lars

Wynne

Hal

Siân

Mike

The Waiter

THE MENU

Aperitif

The Starter
Primordial Soup

The Main
Apocalypse of Lobster

The Dessert
Frozen Waste

The Cheeseboard

DINNER

Scene One

APERITIF

A table set for a lavish dinner, surrounded by darkness.
A Waiter stands on the edge of the light. He is formally
dressed and holds a chic floral arrangement.
    Paige enters, dramatically attired.

Paige Am I paying you to stand there?
    Yes, I think I am. Don't move

    She approaches the Waiter.

Everything you represent thrills me.
    May I?

    She kisses him. She puts a thickly stuffed envelope
    into his pocket.

Your fee
    It's all in advance as we arranged
    There won't be any tip
    So I'm relying on you to serve with grace
    In silence.
    When the time comes

    She is interrupted.

Could you put that on the table, please?

    Lars enters, wearing a casual linen suit. The Waiter
    places the floral arrangement on the table. Lars is
    examining his trousers.

Lars I've got something on here

Paige (*to the Waiter*) In the middle

Lars Some sort of / crusty stuff

3

Paige That's not the middle

The Waiter moves the floral arrangement.

The success of my evening depends on you. So prove capable. I hope your instructions are clear

The Waiter bows. He exits.

Lars I think it might be the cat

Paige Where?

Lars There, on the leg
  It's made a stain

Paige Well, it doesn't show

Lars Maybe I should change them

Paige You always do this to me!

Lars What?

Paige I am perfectly in control of the situation. You come in harassing me with your pathetic frets and I start to panic

Lars What about?

Paige The starter

Lars What's wrong with it?

Paige They might not understand its subtlety

Lars Your starters are always fantastic

Paige Don't / mollify me

Lars And even if they hate it you can tell them that the main will be well worth the wait

Paige I want the main to be a surprise. I want it to confound them!

Lars Well / I'm sure it

Paige It's already ruined by that friend of yours being a vegetarian

The Waiter enters with modish cruets. He places them on the table.

Lars Her name's Wynne

Paige It's ludicrous coming to dinner saying, 'I can't eat anything that's been alive!' She should be eating granite because even the bunny food I'm serving up for her was once alive. It wasn't sentient; it didn't have a soul but it photosynthesised. Perhaps I'll point that out

Lars That would make her feel welcome, wouldn't it?

Paige (*to the Waiter*) We need drinks

The Waiter exits.

I know this meal's about your amazing brilliant success and everything, Lars, but it's my statement. It's my creation – like Frankenstein's monster

Lars is fiddling with his stain.

Will you listen!
   I don't live in the fabulous world of profound ideas like you do and food
   It takes on a character
   It looms
   I've had sleepless nights
   With this meal, I'm going to –
   Where *is* everyone, I said seven-thirty!

Lars I expect they've got caught in the fog

Paige It's so *rude* to be late

Lars It's very foggy. I looked out of the window when I was dressing and I could hardly see the pool house

Paige It shows a distinct apathy about coming, a real reluctance, as if they'd rather be in a Little Chef. They're probably sick with dread. God, if I thought they were going to snub us, I'd kill myself

Lars What with?

Paige A pump-action automatic shotgun

Lars What's wrong with pills?

> *She stares at him. The Waiter enters with drinks.*
> *He approaches Paige. She takes one. He approaches*
> *Lars. He takes the other.*

Paige You
Are

Lars You're a tad overdressed, my love

> *The doorbell rings.*

There. The fog has safely spewed up a guest

> *Lars is on his way to answer it.*

Paige Let the waiter go

Lars I can get it

Paige It's his job

> *The Waiter crosses the stage and exits.*

Lars Did you get him from the usual place?

Paige No, I found him on the internet. He had his own website

Lars A waiter with a website?

Paige It was very well designed. I was intrigued by the wording

Lars What wording?

Paige It said let me hold your coat and snicker

Lars So you don't know him?

Paige Not intimately acquainted

Lars Did you check his references?

Paige They were excellent. He's a man of experience

Wynne enters, taking off cycling paraphernalia. She hands it all to the Waiter. Underneath, she is dressed in Bohemian style.

Wynne God, I'm so sorry; the fog is unbelievable! I had to cycle right down the middle of the road so I could see the white line

Lars Goodness

Wynne And I was really feeling watched, you know, as if there were eyes hidden in the mist, when this moron in a Saab zoomed by and sent me swerving right into one of those gryphon things on your gateposts

Lars You poor thing

Wynne Really knocked my knee

Lars Oh no

Lars hugs her. She kisses him on the lips.

Wynne It's so good to see you

Lars This is my wife, Paige

Paige Hello, Wynne

Wynne Paige, lovely to meet you

She kisses Paige on the cheek. The Waiter exits with Wynne's things.

Paige Lars said you were bringing your other half

Lars Bob

Paige I'm terribly excited

Wynne Don't be

Paige I adore politicians. The last one I met came to the door at election time. He was so persuasive I almost had his child

Wynne Um, he's in the pub

Paige I'm sorry?

Wynne Bob.
    I'm afraid he's not coming

Paige I'm devastated

Wynne Oh

Paige He was vitally important to my interesting mix of guests

Wynne We've had a bit of a –
    We've just parted company

Lars Wynne, are you OK?

The Waiter enters.

Wynne He's been seeing someone behind my back

Lars Oh no

Wynne Her name's Pam

Lars That's *awful*

Wynne She's a temp with a crush. It's so tacky

Lars You poor thing

Wynne Don't be nice to me or I'll cry

Paige You didn't think of phoning me?

Wynne Pardon?

Paige To tell me that Bob had a new girlfriend and wasn't going to come?

Wynne I –

Lars Of course she didn't

Paige Only I have odd numbers now and a spare main, which is a terrible waste. It'll probably rot in the fridge

Wynne I'm sorry but this has *just happened*. (*to Lars*) I found a letter. She called him Bobble

Lars You're joking

Wynne She said he made her quiver like a jelly

Lars What a cliché

Wynne She had writing like a child and she signed herself Cuddly Pam

Paige Were you rooting through his personal belongings?

Wynne Only his coat! He tried to tell me that Pam was a harmless fantasy fulfilment and why was I getting so het up? I said a harmless *what*? He said she was so –
 Can I sit down somewhere?

Lars Of course, sorry

Wynne So young

Paige (*to the Waiter*) She needs a chair

Lars I'll get one

Paige It's his job

> The Waiter fetches a chair from the table. He arranges it for Wynne. Wynne sits.

Wynne Thank you

Paige We need drinks

Wynne It's in response
He's never forgiven me for –
It was when I put my portrait of his genitals in my
exhibition
I'd painted it from memory
Vigorous
And there was purple
Perhaps I should have called the picture something else
but I thought why not call it 'Bob Patterson's Cock'?
That's what it is

Paige (*to the Waiter*) I said drinks

The Waiter exits.

Wynne He said how could you, it's nothing like mine
I said it's impressionistic
He said look at my balls; they're falling off
I said that's a dreamlike quality
A cartoon appeared in the opposition newsletter
The Member for Camberwell Green
I meant it as a gesture!

*The Waiter enters with drinks on a tray. He
approaches Wynne. She takes one.*

He said I was trying to castrate him
I said Bob
I'm not a feminist I'm an eroticist I'm free about
everything I don't hold back I did it to share why
shouldn't I share my feelings with the world?
He said why shouldn't I share mine with Pam?
He was triumphant
I said no wonder she called you Bobble. Your cock's /
like a

Lars The man's a fool. (*as a toast*) Here's to freedom

Wynne Freedom

Lars clinks glasses with Wynne.

Paige I'll drink to that.

Wynne Lars, I love your book, I really, really love it. It's like everything I've always thought only I haven't known I've thought it
Honestly, I read it and I just thought, 'Yes!' It was so –
I mean I know I've known you for ever but it's made me feel –
Oh goodness
Every time I think of it I know I'm strong

Lars Well, I –

Wynne Paige, isn't it brilliant?

Paige I haven't read it

Wynne Pardon?

Paige I thought I'd wait till it came out in paperback. Then I wouldn't worry if I dropped it in the bath

Lars She thinks of everything

Paige I'm just going to put that spare main away for the cat. (*to the Waiter*) Would you come with me? I want to discuss the dessert

Paige exits, followed by the Waiter.

Wynne It's genius, Lars, honestly. I was blown away

Lars I'm glad he didn't come

Wynne The psychological apocalypse is such a brilliant concept
Putting a name like that to what so many of us feel

I mean, it's obvious you've been through things
You know
Suffered

Lars Oh

Wynne You write with such insight

Lars Thank you

Wynne And your new morality thrilled me. It's so bold
You've said what we all think but daren't utter
Refusing to be dragged down by write-offs
Oh . . .To walk away from the choking weeds that failed us
To free oneself from liability, from blame –
We think it must be shameful
But you're right. It's a powerful force

Lars Be the Phoenix

Wynne I'm regendering myself right now. This stuff about Bob; it's just a negative influxion, isn't it?

Lars That's right

Wynne I can deflect it

Lars You certainly can

Wynne Overcome it even at the point of wound entry

Lars You look wonderful

Wynne No I don't. I'm all splodgy and cryey

Lars Think what the woman who'd read my book would say

Wynne She'd say yes
I look wonderful
Thank you

Lars You're shining

Wynne Lars

Lars An embodiment
Of everything alive

*They kiss: illicit, passionate, full of promise. The
doorbell rings. They separate as the Waiter enters.
He crosses the stage; exits. Paige enters with a drink.*

Paige Well this must be Hal and Siân. They're great fun
He's a scientist; works in the cutting-edge arena of
germs
He used to be married to my best friend Mags but he
left her
And now he's married to Siân
She's a sexpot

*Hal and Siân enter. He wears a seen-better-days jacket
and tie; she is stunning in black. The Waiter follows
them. He takes their coats.*

Paige Hello newlyweds, lovely to see you

Lars Come in, come in

Hal We have just had the worst journey. Thought we
weren't going to bloody get here. The fog is unbelievable

Wynne God yes it's / terrible isn't –

Lars Couldn't see the pool earlier

Hal Couldn't see your drive. Been going up and down
that lane for about half an hour. Nearly knocked some
mad witch off a bike and I don't know how we're going
to get home. You might be stuck with us all night, Paige!

Paige What fun. (*to the Waiter*) We need drinks

The Waiter exits.

Hal Do you know there was a moment when I thought
this is getting really Stephen King, as if any minute Jack

13

Nicholson was going to appear going – (*He laughs an insane laugh.*) – with a big bloodspattered axe and then the windscreen would shatter and – (*He throttles himself.*) – curtains. It's really spooky out there. More than spooky; überspooky

Siân I expect he's busy getting fat

Hal Who?

Siân Jack Nicholson

Hal What?

Lars Hal, this is Wynne

Wynne Hello, super

Hal Great pleasure

Lars Siân, Wynne

Siân Hi

Wynne Nice to meet you

Lars Wynne and I go way back. We were actually at college together and we lost touch for years and years, then, just a short time ago, I decided to go to this life-drawing class and lo and behold, amazing coincidence, Wynne was teaching it

Wynne I couldn't believe it when he walked in. He was exactly the same. Except for the badges

Lars Do you want to know the truth?
  I found out you were teaching it before I went

Wynne Did you?

Lars I'd been to your exhibition the week before

Wynne Why didn't you tell me?

Lars I thought it was brilliant

The Waiter enters with drinks. He serves them.

Hal So what do you exhibit?

Lars She's an artist

Paige Sadly undiscovered as yet

Hal Right

Wynne Probably because I'm figurative

Hal That's bowls of fruit and stuff, isn't it?

Lars It means she can paint. She doesn't just make crap out of crap and call it art

Paige Do you know anything about art, Siân?

Siân Yes

Wynne So, what do you like?

Siân I like the graffiti on the back of toilet doors. I saw some today that said Fuck Shit Up. Is that art?

Paige It's literature

Wynne Do you know I've got a really funny feeling that I've met you somewhere before

Siân Right

Wynne I wasn't being funny or –

Hal You've seen her on the goggle box

Wynne Are you an actress?

Siân I'm a journalist

Hal She's a newsbabe. Aren't you, love?

Siân (*pause*) I'm a newsbabe

Wynne That's right!

Siân I decorate the rolling news

Hal Don't do yourself down

Wynne That is such a scary job. It must be awful when things go wrong

Hal Oh, she thrives on it. Sits there with a smile on her face and drops the other presenter in it

Wynne I'd be absolutely hopeless at it

Paige Yes

Wynne And gosh – it must cost you a fortune in suits

Siân I get an allowance
Can I smoke in here?

Paige You feel free. I'll spray around in the morning. (*to the Waiter*) Ashtray

The Waiter exits.

Hal So
You've really done it with this book then

Lars I don't know

Hal Oh, you have. You've really effing blinding done it. You're for sale on a special stand in John effing Menzies that's how much you've done it

Lars Well the reviews haven't *all* been good

Paige Have you read it, Hal?

Hal Yes
Yes
I read it

Lars And?

Hal Great
Loved it

Lars You don't have to lie

Hal No, I did
Life-changing
Really tip-top

The Waiter enters with an ashtray. He stands near Siân, holding it out for her use.

Siân He said it was as dry as old dog biscuits

Hal I did not

Siân But he was freaked / couldn't finish it

Hal Leave it, honeybunch

Siân He thought it was too nihilistic or something.
I thought it was a smorgasbord of syllogisms that
ultimately ate itself, but that's only the opinion of a
newsbabe, Lars, so I wouldn't take it to heart

Paige (*to the Waiter*) What are you doing with that? She
doesn't want to stand there and flick ash on you

Siân I'll put it out

Paige No! Why don't you find something to stand it on?

*The Waiter removes the ashtray just as Siân goes to
stub her cigarette out. It falls to the floor.*

Siân Sorry

She grinds it out with her foot.

Paige Waiter
Fuck shit up

The Waiter exits.

Well here we all are. I'd just like to say welcome,
tremendous congratters for getting through the fog and
sorry that we're odd numbers. Wynne's lover has just
dumped her and can't attend

Hal Oh bad luck

Wynne 'S fine / 's nothing

Paige So that leaves just the four of us to toast Lars and his remarkable achievement in modern philosophy: for the third week running he's outsold Delia Smith's *Cooking for the Brain Dead*. To Lars

Hal Well done, mate

Siân Yep

Wynne To you

   The Waiter enters with a dustpan and brush.

Lars Thank you all very much. It's actually quite humbling that my book, arguably syllogistic as I'm sure it is, should have tapped the twenty-first century zeitgeist in / quite such a

Paige Well, our starter awaits, quivering in its prime Waiter, when you've dealt with that we'd like to sit

   The Waiter nods. He sweeps up the ash.

Wynne He's very professional, isn't he?

Paige I hope so

Wynne Does he do the hoovering too?

Paige No

Lars Paige found him on the internet

Wynne Oh, I'm an internet virgin, a total Luddite. I hate the whole idea of it

Paige You don't know what you're missing

Wynne So alienating

Paige You can find anything you want on the internet, from plumbers and hired assassins right through to Siamese-twin prostitutes who'll dance naked in front of your friends

Hal Is that what you've arranged for later?

Paige No

Hal Shame
   Ha!

The Waiter exits with the dust pan and brush.

Wynne Lars has told me all about your dinners, Paige

Hal Oh, they're famous

Lars She is indeed an artist of the Aga

Wynne I can't wait. I feel very honoured to be invited

Paige Well, it was Bob I really wanted to meet

Wynne Oh

Lars She's attempting a negative influxion

Wynne Ah, well then
   Deflected

Paige (*to Wynne*) Wynne, would you like to freshen up before we eat? I can lend you a clean pair of tights

Wynne (*looking down at her laddered tights, dismayed*) Oh –

Paige And Siân, you probably want some mouthwash

Siân I'd like a piss actually

Paige Super. We've got two little girls' rooms; you can have one each. And we'll leave you boys to discuss the crisis in masculinity

Paige, Wynne and Siân exit.

Hal Nice to see Paige on form

Lars Yes

Hal You still haven't have told her, then?

Lars No

Hal Right. Tough business

Lars How did you do it with Mags?

Hal Sorry, mate; can't go there

The Waiter enters with crockery for soup. He sets it at the table.

That's not what I thought, by the way. About your book.
Siân can really put words / in my mouth

Lars Doesn't matter

Hal Well look. I'm going to admit
    I didn't like the whole – I mean what? – psychological
apocalypse thing. And the way it's being marketed like
some kind of effing bible when it's called
    I mean I just don't think you can make a bible out of
lack of belief

Lars I'm not trying to

Hal Oh, come on

Lars I'm not

Hal Look
    I know that we're born for no reason and survive by
accident
    I know it every time I look down a microscope and see
    Dumb organisms
    Vacuously multiplying, gormlessly devouring, pointlessly
expiring

A hideous human death in each one of them like –
Like things you couldn't make up in a nightmare

Lars You need to get out of the lab, Hal

Hal What I'm saying is it's not your nihilism I take issue
with

Lars I'm not nihilistic

Hal It's your –
Do you know
I think I hate it because you're probably right
Anyway
Been feeling a bit mad lately and that sort of you
know –
Probably just jealous. I mean, my book's been lying
around covered in mildew in the section marked 'Geeks'
for effing years

Lars We're alone in an uncaring universe, Hal

Hal Holy batcrap

Lars And the world is a mad cacophony of excess. Every
living thing is either consuming or in a state of decay.
You're right, we're no better than microbes. You can
dwell on the fact that our lives have no meaning for as
long as you like. You can dwell on life's pain and life's
injustice. You can latch on to all that negativity like a big
sour tit. That kind of thinking leads to the inevitable –

Hal OK

Lars To the psychological apocalypse

Hal So we all go crazy

Lars We perceive the truth of our condition
Yes, that truth is painful
And yes, if one dwells on it in isolation one could go
mad

Hal Ha

Lars But
What I have done for those who reach that point
That abyss
Is to offer a choice, a cure if you like

Hal Physician, heal thyself

Lars I say the psychological apocalypse is a cosmic wake-up call. And a position of total despair is a great place to wake from because, Hal, the only way is up

Hal There's always down. Things can always, always be worse

Lars Would you rather consume, or rot? To go back to your microbe analogy, that is the central question. Do you want to eat or have things eat you?

Hal The whole thing comes down to power for you, doesn't it?

Lars Power sounds supremacist and my philosophy is not. I call it psyche-drive. With the psyche-drive of the will, you can decide to live and flourish or you can decide to rot

Paige appears at the door. She listens, unnoticed except by the Waiter.

Hal You want us to behave like diseases

Lars No

Hal Well, it's just capitalism gone mad then, isn't it? Consume / consume

Lars No, no

Hal And the thing about consumption is that once your host organism is completely devoured – and in our case the host is the planet Earth – once / it's consumed, you rot anyway!

Lars I'm not talking about consumption on a physical level; I'm talking about psyche-attitude. People let themselves putrefy. Look at Mags

Hal Could you just not go there?

Lars Well, look at Paige then

Hal Paige is the ultimate consumer

Lars Oh, look harder; she's decomposing

Hal So anyone who professes to any pain or weakness is decomposing?

Lars It's their decision: do they indulge or deflect?

Hal What about the meek?

Lars The who?

Hal The unfashionable meek: the selfless, the givers. Blessed are they, Lars

Lars Oh bullshit

Hal For theirs is the Kingdom of Heaven

Lars You don't believe that

Hal I believe that there's virtue in / compassion

Lars As Heaven doesn't exist, the meek are very welcome to it. And so is anyone else who'd rather be dead than alive. I say you can leave pain behind. And I don't lack compassion. My lessons on psyche-drive and negative deflection come directly from the Buddha

Hal So this new way of thinking, this Nazi Buddhist morality

Lars I object to Nazi

Hal How is it for you? In your own life? Not for the superman persona who's obviously written your book / but for you?

Lars There is nothing Nazi in my thinking. How dare you suggest it?

Hal Anyway, answer my question will you because I can't believe that you can simply decide to walk away from life's pain and find yourself free

Lars Look at me, Hal. You know me of old

Hal You're the guy who can see gaps in the despair market

Lars Do I seem different to you?
Am I raging? Sulking?
Am I agonising over people I'm powerless to change?
I'm cool Hal

Hal You always were

Lars My friend
You've spent your life exploring every avenue of thought
You're a deep-thinking man

Hal Yes

Lars For your own good
Abandon it

Hal You want me to abandon thought?

Lars This self-absorbed negativity. You're drowning in it. You've spent long enough allowing the meek to tyrannise you. It's time to stop, to let them go

The Waiter is still, looking at Paige.

Haven't you got anything to do?

The Waiter looks at Lars. He exits.

24

Hal So without all this, um
    Thought
    What am I left with?

Lars Peace

Hal OK

Lars Freedom

Hal Right

Lars And passion

Hal Uh-huh

Lars The eternal moment of present. Hal, in order to heal you simply abandon yourself to our most powerful instinct, the instinct of I Want. You abandon yourself to the sensual world

Hal I see
    I was hoping you wouldn't say that

Lars Why?

Hal I tried it
    Doesn't fucking work

Scene Two

THE STARTER

The diners are seated at the table. The Waiter is serving with impeccable grace, ladling from a stylish tureen. Everyone but Paige is unnerved by the colour and texture of the soup. The Waiter finishes serving.

Paige We need drinks

The Waiter nods. He exits.
The diners tentatively start to eat. The soup is disgusting. Only Paige manages to swallow it without extreme difficulty.

I saw Mags the other day, Hal

Hal Great

Paige She's doing really well. They're allowing her into a halfway house. She might be home in a month or two

Hal Yes

Paige And she says the scars look so much better. She's going to have reconstructive surgery

Hal I know

Paige Oh yes, you're paying for it, aren't you? She was telling me how lovely and generous you've been. She really appreciated That Card

Hal involuntarily gags. The Waiter enters with drinks. He serves them.

Paige (*referring to the empty chair*) The invisible guest. No dinner party is complete without one. When we were newlyweds, Lars and I used to have a joke at our dinners. If a guest didn't arrive, we always called the empty seat Jesus' chair

Lars No we didn't

Paige Because I used to say what a great dinner guest Jesus would be. Lars said he didn't think he could bear entertaining someone who wore sandals, but I thought he'd be witty and provocative and offer interesting carpentry tips. He'd also provide great entertainment raising the food from the dead and whathaveyou

Hal Paige, Siân's a Christian

Siân No I'm not

Hal Yes you are

Siân I am not

Hal She's a Christian

Siân Christ

Paige I genuinely think Jesus would be a thrilling guest in all but one way

Siân And what's that?

Paige He'd hold us up to judgement. And who'd want that? We'd all get indigestion

Wynne Is there, um
  Any meat in this, Paige?

Paige Oh no. Lars told me you existed solely on vegetable matter and I absolutely respect that

Wynne There's, um
  A flavour I can't put my finger on

Paige Well, I suppose there might be the odd zoo-plankton in there – but they're pretty hard to eliminate in this dish. Would you object to eating zoo-plankton?

Wynne I don't know

Paige They're single cell animals so I suppose technically they're meat. I could have the waiter blast it in the microwave for you, then at least you'd know they were dead

Lars What is this, Paige?

Paige It's soup, my love. Lars loves traditional-type starters. He can't be doing with mimsy salads and little piles of swept-up, drizzled-on chicken bits. He calls those kind of starters goat poo, don't you?

Lars No

Paige He likes something substantial and as this meal is entirely in his honour I'd thought I'd pull out all the stops

Wynne What's in it?

Paige It's an onion, celeriac and parsnip base, with algae

Wynne Algae?

Paige Simmered slowly at a very low temperature, in brine

Hal That would account for the salt, then

Paige There's a bouquet garni in there and a dash of sulphur – which might be that indefinable flavour, Wynne

Siân Is it one of those Nigella Lawson things?

Paige Oh no; it's such a simple dish. The only thing that's tricky is getting the temperature to stay low enough – and the cooking time

Siân Right

Paige Three weeks
    I was pulling my hair out thinking how can I cook this without Lars knowing? How can I keep it as a special

surprise? And I came up with a genius solution. I put the pan on the sunbed out in the summerhouse. That way, it's had not only heat, but light to photosynthesise. I've been out there to stir it every other day and about a week ago I added a sprinkling of yeast

Lars Well, that's remarkable, Paige

Paige It's called Primordial Soup

Hal Great

Paige The living starter. Enjoy

Wynne involuntarily gags.

Siân It must be Gordon Ramsay

Paige As a matter of fact, Siân, after a great deal of research and experimentation, I wrote the recipe myself

Lars I'd have expected nothing less

Paige Then I haven't let you down

The diners continue in their efforts to eat the soup.

This soup is actually in honour of you, Hal

Hal Is it?

Paige (*to Wynne*) Hal is a world expert on microbes

Wynne Oh

Paige He wrote a fascinating book a number of years ago called *The Microbe Within*. It was very informative; lovely diagrams – but it didn't quite get that Nobel Prize, did it, Hal?

Hal No, Paige, it didn't

Wynne What are you working on at the moment?

Hal It's not interesting

Wynne I'm sure it is. I'm mesmerised by science. Everyone's saying it's the new art

Hal Really?

Wynne It would be so easy for you to make art out of your job and for me to make science out of mine

Hal Would it?

Wynne Oh yes. You could do an exhibition of microbes you know; project magnified images or paint representations of them breeding or eating other microbes or whatever microbes do. Because I'm sure – and I'll bet a lot of people don't think about this – that when you're close up to microbes, they're actually rather beautiful

Hal I've never thought about their aesthetic

Wynne And I could do the science of art with prisms and things. The boundaries between art and science are almost non-existent these days, don't you think, Hal?

Hal Sure

Wynne What exactly are you working on?

Hal It's really not interesting

Lars (*to the Waiter*) Could we have some Parmesan cheese?

Paige You'll spoil it

Lars I'd like some Parmesan cheese

The Waiter exits.

Siân (*to Wynne*) He's studying the microbes in sheepshit

Hal That's not what I'm doing

Siân If it's not sheepshit it's pigshit or something

Hal That Is Not What I Am Doing

Wynne You know that's why I would never ever eat meat. We just don't know what's in it these days. Are you looking for mutancy and hideous diseases?

Hal No

The Waiter enters with Parmesan cheese. He serves Lars.

Wynne Because we pump them full of hormones and steroids and antibiotics, we feed them on bone slurry and keep them in cages where they develop muscular atrophy and drink each others' urine. Even seafood is caged now. Do you know, they're trying to breed de-sexed crabs so they don't go mad and kill each other in their overcrowded farming tanks and they're covered in vile moulds and sea lice and their eyes are all cataracted and –

Paige The main course is seafood

Wynne Oh

Paige So, a lot to look forward to

Hal My work has nothing to do with sheep or cows or any other farmyard animal, Wendy. That's just Siân's little joke

The Waiter is offering Wynne Parmesan cheese.

Paige (*to the Waiter*) What are you doing with that? No one else wants it

Siân I'll have some

Paige Take it away

The Waiter exits.

Wynne So what are you doing, Hal? Or do you just not want to talk about it?

Hal I'd love to talk about it, Wendy. But I can't

Wynne You don't have to be embarrassed

Hal I've signed the Official Secrets Act

Wynne Oh

Lars He works for the Government

Wynne Oh my God

Hal In a minor capacity

Wynne Biological warfare

Hal What on earth makes you say that?

Wynne Well I don't know
James Bond and things

Hal How could this country possibly be involved in something like that?

Wynne Well, I'm sure it's not, but –

Hal But nothing. It isn't. And neither am I

Wynne I wasn't being serious. I mean, I hope you don't think I'm some sort of, you know, anti-whatnot person

Siân Hal's very touchy about his work

Hal As a matter of fact, Wendy, I work for the Ministry of Health

Siân Torturing lab rats

Hal Why are you –
I mean what is the –

Siân What?

Hal Is this because I called you a newsbabe?

Siân No

Hal Because that was a joke. It was an effing joke, OK?

Siân Sure, whatever

Hal Meet Siân, everybody. She's a *journalist*. She wants you all to know that her skill at reading an autocue has nothing to do with the way she looks

Siân lights a cigarette.

Wynne Um, Hal, my name isn't Wendy

Hal What?

Wynne You called me Wendy just then and my name's actually Wynne

Hal I'm so sorry. Wynne

The doorbell rings.

Lars Are we expecting anyone else?

Paige No

Lars (*getting up*) No biblical figures or Siamese twins?

Paige Sadly not

Wynne It might be Bob

Paige Let the waiter go

Lars I can get it

Paige It's his job

The Waiter enters. He crosses the stage and exits.

Paige Would anyone like any more? The great thing about this dish is that the leftovers breed, so you never completely run out. Hal, can I tempt you?

Hal I'm saving myself for the main

Paige The other extraordinary thing about this starter is that it creates its own oxygen. If you were to take it to

Mars, lift the lid of the tureen and come back in a billion years or so, you'd find you were stepping into a new Eden. This soup is an irrepressible force of life. And that's why I wanted to share it with you all. When we're surrounded by so much excess I think it's wonderful to remember that we were once such persistent slime

Lars Bravo

Siân Slime is the agony of water

Hal What?

Siân Sartre

Hal What?

> *Mike is shown in by the Waiter. He's in his twenties, wearing nondescript clothes. He seems to be waiting for the Waiter to speak.*

Lars Can we help you?

Mike Um, I asked him if I could borrow a phone. I've had an accident down on the lane and –

> *Siân turns. Mike sees her.*

Oh my God. You're thing
Off the news
You were on this morning

Siân Yes

Mike That bit about cluster bombs

Siân Right

Mike They're fucking evil, aren't they?

Siân Yes

Paige Who are you and what do you want?

Mike Um, just a phone. Um, my van . . . It's gone into your gatepost. I'm very sorry but I just couldn't see. / I came out of the corner and –

Wynne Oh, you poor thing

Mike I'm really sorry to bother you but I need to use a phone. (*to Siân*) I can't believe you're in here. I must be concussed

Paige Have you damaged our property?

Mike I think my van came out worse. But one of those eagle things you've got on your gates fell off and I think it's broken its nose

Paige Its beak

Wynne He's bleeding

Mike If you could just let me use a phone

Wynne From his cheek, look

Mike I need to call out a tow truck

Paige Waiter?
  Show him the door

Lars Paige?

Paige There's a phone box down by the traffic lights. I suggest you use that

Lars What?

Wynne He's cut himself

Paige He's damaged our property

Lars The man only wants to make a phone call

Paige (*to the Waiter*) Show him out

35

Lars No. He can make his call and sit in the warmth while he waits for help

Mike Look, I'll go

Lars No

Mike I / don't want to cause

Lars It's no problem

Paige Show him out

Lars (*to Paige*) What's the matter with you? Waiter, take his coat

Mike It's OK, I'll go

Paige Show him out!

Lars Take his coat!

Paige (*to the Waiter*) Remember what you're here for and be very, very careful what you do

Lars Why don't you join us? / There's a spare place here. Take the weight off your feet and the waiter will bring you a phone in a minute

Paige You've walked in on a very special party. You haven't been invited and I think you should leave

Lars He's not leaving this house until we've helped him!

Mike Actually, I'm going

Paige Very sensible

Lars NO, TAKE HIS COAT NOW

Mike Really, I'm –

Lars SIT DOWN

 Pause.

Paige Waiter, would you take the gentleman's coat before my husband reaches apoplectic collapse?

The Waiter removes Mike's coat.

Mike I only want to / use a phone; I'll be

Paige We need drinks

The Waiter exits.

May we know your name?

Mike Mike

Paige Well, Mike
I'm Paige
This is Lars, my husband, who hasn't lost his temper since 1999
And these are our guests: Wynne, she's an artist, Hal, a very famous microbiologist, and his wife Siân, who you know

Siân Hi

Mike Hi

Hal Bad luck about your van

Wynne (*getting up*) Mike, you've got to let me look at that cut for you

Mike It's OK

Wynne Paige, have you got an Elastoplast?

Paige No. Tonight, Mike, we're having a little party; just a few close friends to celebrate the successful publication of my husband's book

Mike Right

Paige You might have heard of it. It's called *Beyond Belief*

Mike Is it a thriller?

Paige Lars, is it a thriller?

Lars No

Wynne It's a guidebook, Mike, a guidebook to life

Hal Modern philosophy, mate

Mike Oh, I know. Like one o' them *Armchairs of the Gods* books

Lars I'm sorry?

Wynne is fussing over Mike's cut with her napkin.

Mike (*flinching*) Um, I'm fine

Wynne It must hurt terribly

Mike It's OK

Wynne Poor you

Paige Lars?

Lars What?

Paige What do you suppose Mike means by *Armchairs of the Gods*? Do you think he might be equating your insightful philosophical text with the 'Aliens Built the Pyramids' genre?

Lars I'm sure Mike doesn't mean any offence

Paige What if he does?

Lars Why would he?

Paige Would you still want him to stay?

Lars (*standing*) Paige
I have a request

Paige What's that, my love?

Pause.

Lars (*to Mike*) Make yourself at home, mate
Excuse me

Lars exits. Wynne goes to follow him.

Paige (*to Wynne*) Where are you going?

Wynne Well . . . is he all right?

Paige He's in shock. Helping Mike is the first altruistic thing he's done since he adopted a penguin at London Zoo for my birthday last year. I expect he's gone to fetch you all our jewels and valuables

Mike What d'you mean?

Paige Well, that is why you're here, isn't it?

The Waiter enters with drinks. He serves them.

Mike I don't understand why you'd say that

Paige What do you want?

Mike I just want a phone. My van's / gone into –

Paige That's the most stupid story I've ever heard

Mike You can go out and look

Paige And find the place ransacked when we get back?

Mike Why would I want to ransack your place?

Paige Well, everyone wants something, Mike

Mike If I'd come to steal from you, why would I knock on the door? I'd go round the back, wouldn't I, and break in

Paige Would you now?

Mike I rang your bell; he let me in. If you didn't want strangers in here you should've told him

Paige No one blows in here off the street

Mike And if you tell him to bring me back my coat / I'll put it on and go

Paige What do you want?

Hal Paige, he's just a kid

Mike My name is Mike
My van's in a ditch
I asked for simple help
Fuck, I should of known better asking from people like you
What a waste o' time

Paige What do you mean, people like us?

Mike Rich cunts

Wynne Oh, I can't bear that word

Hal No call for that, mate. You'd better steady on

Paige Less than one minute and he's held us up to judgement
He's worse than Jesus

The Waiter is offering Mike and Paige drinks.

Mike Could I have my coat back, please?

Paige You don't really want to leave, do you?

Mike I want my coat

Paige Take a drink first

Mike No thank you

Paige Go on

Mike Would you get me my coat, please?

Paige Join us for a drink, Mike

Mike Why?

Paige See how the rich cunts live

Hal Paige
Give him his coat and let him go

Paige Pick one up
Sip it
It's like ambrosia
The gods themselves drink stuff like this
Sitting in their armchairs

Mike takes a drink.

Bravo

*Paige takes one. She clinks Mike's glass. They drink.
Mike downs his in one. He wipes his mouth.*

Mike Babycham

Paige I'd like you to join us for dinner

Hal Oh, come on

Paige Why have an empty seat in the pleasuredome
when we could extend a benevolent hand to a stranger?
It's what Lars wants. Mike, on his behalf, I'm inviting
you to join us

Mike No thank you

Paige Why not?

Mike I couldn't

Paige Have you eaten already?

Mike I'm not hungry

Paige That doesn't matter

Mike I'd rather sit in my van

Paige It's no imposition

Mike I wouldn't care if it was

Paige That's why I'm inviting you

Mike I might pick your pockets

Paige This outfit doesn't have them
      You won't get a tow truck for hours in all that fog.
You might as well stay

Siân Come on, sit down. The food's great

Hal What?

Paige There's even a place set for you

Siân Jesus' chair

Paige Take it. We're all dying to know if you think we're
redeemable

Wynne Mike, look. I'd be very happy for you to stay
but I really object to that word that you just said

Mike Then I'm sorry for saying it

Paige Wynne hates anyone calling her rich

Mike I see

Paige So that's settled. You'll stay

Mike Well, I could try to make a dash for it but
(*referring to the Waiter*) I don't think I'd get past him.
You got me trapped, Paige

Paige Mike
      Welcome to dinner

Scene Three

THE MAIN

Mike is seated at the table with the other diners. The soup dishes have been cleared. The Waiter is laying out all the equipment needed for the consumption of lobsters.

Mike So when I came out of the army I didn't really know what to do with myself. All my friends were going into full-time alcoholism or the prison service but I knew that wasn't for me, so I started up this business doing removals, deliveries, property relocation, that kind of thing

Wynne That's amazing

Mike Not really

Wynne You're an entrepreneur

Mike More of a van driver

Hal So what's the most interesting thing you've ever had in the back of your van, Mike? Apart from your girlfriend, of course

Mike Well, Hal, this one guy I was helping was a reptile freak and he had a collection of snakes and lizards and this chameleon, which really did change colour. Its eyes swivelled round; it had feet like pincers and a tongue like a coiled spring

Hal Bit like Siân

Mike It was the most amazing living thing I've ever seen

Paige We need drinks

The Waiter exits.

Wynne Do you miss the army, Mike?

Mike I liked the travel, but in the end I was glad to leave. I think you reach a certain point when the idea of killing lots of people just loses its appeal. Anyway, Siân, what about you?

Siân What about me?

Mike I mean how did you end up doing what you do?

Siân They just chose me from a photograph

Mike Yeh right

Siân Obviously they had to check I could read. And they did a test to ensure that I didn't have any speech impediments

Mike OK

Siân I had to pronounce words like Shi'ite and Taoiseach, then I had to screen-test with the senior male presenter to satisfy them that we had the right chemistry

Mike Does it get to you?

Siân What?

Mike The news?

Siân How?

The Waiter enters with drinks. He serves them.

Mike You're the first port of call for all the bad news in the world. All day digesting horror and violence and tragedy – I suppose it's no wonder you're detached

Hal She's so detached she's actually floating somewhere in the stratosphere and all we've got here is a hologram

Siân It's not all horror and tragedy. We always do a fun item at the end

Mike Yeh. You pull an item on a massacre or a famine and replace it with the badger who crawled into someone's washing machine

Wynne Oh my –

Siân People don't give a fuck about massacres and famines. They watch the news because they want to be reassured

Mike Reassured what?

Siân That despite the headlines, things are essentially OK. I think it's to do with control. They've got the information; they know the worst and they can deal with it – if they don't dwell on it for more than ten seconds. Which is why it's so important to end with people safe in the knowledge that the badger survived the rinse and spin

Wynne (*relieved*) Oh

Mike So bad news is bad ratings?

Siân Oh yeh, people get traumatised and turn off. They've done research that suggests it's less likely to happen if news is delivered by thinking man's crumpet in a pastel suit. So it's my job to make events on this fucked-up planet more palatable; peppering the horror and tragedy with tales of plucky burrowing mammals

She lights a cigarette. The Waiter exits.

Mike You demolished that cluster bomb guy. You made it sound like everything that came out of his mouth was a fucking lie – and it was. And when you tell us about the lucky badgers you always look like it's making you barf. So I think, despite what you say, you're on the side of truth

45

Siân (*pause*) Thank you

Hal Mike, Siân's up for the Rear of the Year Award. Did you know?

Mike Congratulations

Siân Thanks

Mike If you win, you'll have to read that night's news with your arse

Siân (*bursts out laughing*) I'd love to

Paige (*to Mike, confidentially*) Did I just ask for drinks?

Mike Yes

Paige has already finished hers.

Paige Oh

Hal So Mike, what's in the back of your van today?

Mike Well, I'm just on my way from robbing the house next door, so quite a lot of antiques, couple o' paintings and some jewellery

Only Siân laughs.

No, seriously, when I say I do property removals that's usually without the owner's knowledge or consent

Paige Bravo

Hal You've just robbed next door?

Mike Yeh. Nice place

Lars enters, wearing different trousers. He coolly sits at the table.

Paige So?

Lars Just dived in the pool

Paige And?

Lars And what?

Paige Was it pleasant?

Lars Very. Very calming

Paige Well I'm glad. That's consolation for the fact that we've all been waiting for our main for half an hour now

Lars You should have started without me

Paige Well, seeing as this dinner is in honour of you and your fabulous, brilliant success, I thought that would be a little rude. *Waiter!*

Lars Mike

Mike Hi

Lars Hi. Are they treating you OK?

Mike Very well, thank you

Lars Have you made your phone call?

Mike Yeh

Lars Good

Paige I've invited him to dine with us

Lars Cool

Mike I'm afraid you're stuck with me for a couple of hours. They can't get a tow truck here any sooner

Lars No problem. Long as you like

The Waiter enters.

Paige We need drinks. Then we're ready for the main

The Waiter nods. He exits.

47

Mike was just about to tell us how he's ripped off old Mrs Allingham next door

Lars Oh

Paige Apparently his van is full of swag

Lars That's cool, Mike, really cool

Paige We're all agog with shock

Wynne You haven't, have you?

Mike Haven't what?

Wynne Well you wouldn't just sit there and tell us, would you?

Mike Why not?

Wynne Oh Mike, you're having us on

Mike Why? I'm very proud of what I do

Siân Good

Hal Do you steal from the rich and give to the poor or something?

Mike No, I just flog it and keep the money like anyone else. But I'm proud of my skills

Wynne You're a bit of a tease, aren't you?

Mike I don't think so

Hal So how did you get started, then? What was your first big break in the tea-leaf trade?

Mike Well, I got this perfect training, courtesy of Her Majesty's Armed Forces. I did a lot of surveillance work – stealth training, that kind o' thing – and when I left it seemed a terrible waste not to do something with it

Paige Quite right

Mike The obvious choice was crime. I mean I aim low – just private houses and that – and I don't do anything where I'd have to carry a weapon – even a knife – because I took a sanctity-of-life pledge. After the killing of two Serbs and a Liberian I'm not ever, *ever* –

Wynne You killed a librarian?

Mike A Liberian. Someone from Liberia. It's next to Sierra Leone

Wynne Oh

Mike I witnessed their murder; I've never actually killed anyone myself

Lars Did you take her Klimt?

Mike What?

Lars She has a Klimt in her study, Mrs Allingham. Did you take it?

Mike A what?

Wynne Gustav Klimt. He's a painter, Mike

Mike Oh, that painting

Wynne A provocative eroticist, like me

Mike I thought it was a print

Lars She's assured me on many occasions that it's her most valuable piece

Mike Shit; I hate art. I never know what I'm looking at. I thought it was greeting-card crap. Do you think I should go back for it?

Hal Never revisit the scene of a crime

Mike It's OK. I disabled the alarm and I know she's out. I've been casing the joint all day

The Waiter enters with drinks. He serves them.

Lars Are you going to be doing our joint?

Mike Well, obviously not tonight. I think that'd be a bit ungrateful, don't you?

Lars Yes I do, Mike

Mike But I tell you what, Lars, if you want to stroll over later and get that Klimt yourself, there's nothing to stop you

Lars Why her? There are far better houses on this road; ours for instance

Mike Well I mean they're all something fucking else, aren't they?
     This is gothic-window plastic-pillar heaven
     But after extensive research I discovered that next door it was just one old doll with a lot of nice gear. And it was going great. No hitches at all until the van went into your ditch
     I thought I don't believe it
     I thought just walk away and forget the whole thing
     But it was so thick with fog I couldn't see
     I thought I could go round and round for hours in this
     End up in Timbukfuckingtu
     So I thought find a house, brazen it out, get a tow truck, get a tow, act the innocent and you'll get away with all that stuff, no fucking bother

     The Waiter exits.

Hal Well, you won't now, will you?

Mike Won't I?

Hal I mean, you've just told us all about it, haven't you?

Mike Oh yes, so I have

Hal We could make a citizen's arrest

Mike You're right

Wynne We could tie you to your chair

Mike I'm in big trouble

　Pause.

Paige I'm sorry, are we gawping?

Mike Just a bit

Paige You'll have to excuse us. It's been years since any of us spoke to anyone working class

Lars That's a great story, Mike

Mike Thanks

Lars You'll have to tell us what you really do some time

Mike Well, I just get by, Lars, in a working-class kind of a way

Wynne Mike, my parents were working class

Mike Right

Wynne I'm only middle class because of my education

Mike Right

Paige You could say the same for Lars. He comes from a very deprived background

Lars That's not true

Paige Oh it is. He never shuts up about how deprived he is

Lars There is nothing deprived about my background, Mike

Paige Sorry, I meant depraved

Lars My father was a small-town dentist and my mother was a self-educated chiropodist

Paige Wait for his funny joke about teeth and feet

Lars Paige went to boarding school

Paige Whereas Lars' parents sent him out to work when he was just a child. They forced him to do a paper round and he still bears the emotional scars

Hal Oh come on, you two

Paige Come on what?

Hal You're like a couple of –
    I don't know

Paige Newlyweds?

Mike Lars

Lars Mike

Mike Can I ask you a rude and personal question?

Lars Sure

Mike How did you make all your money?

Paige What makes you think it's his?

Lars Paige had a small trust fund when we married, which I invested for her. She's welcome to have it back at any time – with interest.
    I used to trade in the city

Mike As simple as that?

Lars Making money's as simple as sneezing. You just have to want to do it. And for a while I did. But it began to bore me – just seemed like figures moving around on screens in the end – so a few years ago I retired and went back to my first love: the study of philosophy

Wynne You've achieved so much in your life, Lars. You put the rest of us to shame

Paige (*angrily*) Oh, where is our food?

Paige takes her glass and goes into the kitchen.

Lars Well, I think the important thing about anyone's journey through life – whatever their background – is that they follow / the

Wynne The positive dictates of the psyche-drive and pursue their aspirational fantasies

Mike Is that what it says in your book?

Lars In a word, yes

Siân It's a zingy read, Mike

Hal But you see my point is
  What about the poor sods who aren't up to it? The ones who don't have the talent or the skill to achieve anything?

Wynne Oh, everyone can achieve *something*, Hal

Siân He only read the first couple of chapters

Hal That's not true

Lars If you choose the wrong aspirational fantasy, your failure to achieve it will probably lead you to psychological apocalypse and that's where the process of renewal can begin

Wynne Yes

Siân He should have hung on in there to Part Two – the phoenix rising stuff. He missed the reinstatement of aspirational fantasies as a one-step-up alternate reality

Mike You've lost me

Siân Well, when nothing is real and only language gives things meaning, why should a dream or a fantasy not have the same weight of reality as a real event or relationship? If you put your fantasies close enough to reality, they become achievable – apparently

Mike Right

Paige returns with a full glass and sits.

Paige Everything is perfectly prepared. He's so diligent

Wynne It's all down to the strength of the psyche-drive, Mike. You can make things happen. It's such a liberating concept. I mean you can't deny that we're all at the epicentre of our own universe. What Lars says is, don't be meek about it, don't be humble; you can be the god or the goddess of your own psyche. Action is the key

Mike OK

Wynne A lot us feel scared of action; afraid of instigating change. But *Beyond Belief* will revolutionise your life. All you have to do is say yes to the strength within you and release the spirit of self

Siân Because you're going to die anyway

Wynne Well, yes, but surely you can handle the idea of your own death? I know I can. I've worked through all that fear to a place of
    Inspired Resignation
    And now I feel I can do anything

Mike Sounds great

Lars Here

Lars reaches into his inside pocket.

Have a copy, Mike

He holds out a small blue book. Mike takes it.

54

Mike Well, thank you, Lars. Nice-looking book

Lars (*winks*) Clever marketing

> *The Waiter enters with a raw savoy cabbage on a
> plate.*

Paige Ah, the vegetarian dish

> *The Waiter puts the cabbage down in front of Wynne.*

Wynne Goodness me
What is it?

Paige It's a cabbage. (*to the Waiter*) We need music

> *The Waiter exits.*

Wynne You are so clever
You've made it look as if it hasn't been touched
What have you stuffed it with – or is it a surprise?

Paige I haven't stuffed it with anything
It's raw

Wynne Oh

Paige I thought it was particularly appropriate for you,
Wynne

Lars Why?

Paige It's the ultimate vegetable

Lars Paige, when my patience with your rudeness runs
out –

Paige Yes?

> *Lars is silent.*

You were about to say something, my love.
Was it the beginning of a threat?

Lars I don't make threats

Paige No, action is your name

Lars You're treading a very fine line

Paige Wynne, was I rude?

Wynne I –

Paige Of course not. I wanted something special for you, knowing that you're an artist. If you'll notice, I've had this cabbage in the freezer to simulate the winter frost it naturally endures. It'll melt into diamonds of dew, which the leaves will cradle in their melancholy folds. It's a culinary poem. I felt that to cook it, indeed to prepare it in any way, would be to spoil it. So as an artist, enjoy

Wynne Well

Paige And now for the seafood

> *Wagner. The Waiter enters. He carries two plates. Each of them is holding a huge North Atlantic lobster. They are alive, their claws tied with satin ribbons, presented on a bed of salad. The Waiter serves the ladies.*

Before you ask, this is another of my creations
    Apocalypse of Lobster

> *The Waiter exits. Wynne shrieks, backing away.*

Wynne That one just moved. I saw its thing move!

Paige Of course it moved. It's looking for the North Atlantic.

Wynne Are they living?

Paige I should hope so. I've been nurturing them in the bath all day

> *Wynne whimpers, distressed. The Waiter returns with three more lobsters. He serves the gentlemen.*

Hal Are you expecting us to eat them alive?

Paige Well, you can if you'd like to, Hal

*The Waiter exits, returning almost immediately with
drinks. He serves them.*

Lars What is the meaning of this?

Paige I think it's fitting that Lars, the philosopher whom
we are honouring, should ask the meaning. Perhaps you
can fathom it, my love

Lars I don't intend to try

Paige Then I'll share my gastronomic journey
   I haven't read my husband's book but I have read the
jacket and all his reviews
   There was one – I think it was in the *Hairdresser's
Journal* –
   That said Lars Janssen obviously thinks he's God

Lars Oh shut up

Paige So with this dish I thought we could all imagine
we were Lars and be God. There is the lobster, soft and
naked beneath its defences, as helpless as mankind,
awaiting its final fate

Lars This is pathetic

Paige So, there's a pot of boiling water in the kitchen
and an ornamental pond out there on the patio, which
I've had the waiter fill with brine. If you want your
lobster to live, take it out and release it to its natural
element. If you want to consume it, take it into the
kitchen, put it face first into the boiling water, listen to it
scream, and when it's cooked the waiter will bring it in
for you. You can crack it open, remove its stomach sacs
and intestines and eat it with the attractive salad. That
way lies lobster apocalypse and that way lies salvation.
The choice, ye gods, is yours

57

Mike Wow

Siân scrapes her chair back. She picks up her lobster and walks determinedly towards the kitchen. Wynne stands.

Wynne No!
Don't kill it

Siân Why not?

Wynne It's horrible

Siân Damn right

Siân exits.

Paige (*to the Waiter*) Would you follow your instructions, please?

The Waiter exits to the kitchen. Hal gets up, takes his lobster towards the patio.

Paige Hal, I'm moved by your compassion for these lowly crustaceans

Hal Eff off

He exits.

Paige Mike?

Mike I don't think I could eat this. No offence, Paige, but I generally like my food to look like food

Mike goes out to the patio. Siân returns. She lights a cigarette.

Siân They don't exactly scream; it's more a kind of wail

Wynne Paige this is –
I'm having great difficulty coping with this

Hal and Mike return with empty plates.

Hal It's getting worse out there

Mike You can't see the pond at all

Hal Nearly effing fell in it

Wynne I'm a guest / in your house and

Paige This lobster reminds me of me. Which is why she has to go in the fiery pot

Paige takes her lobster towards the kitchen. Wynne gets up.

Wynne I'd like you to stop!

Paige If you want to stop me you'll have to use force

Lars Leave her

Paige You're the goddess of your own psyche, Wynne

Lars There's no point speaking to her when she's like this

Paige Come and take it. Do something

Wynne I beg you to stop

Paige I despise begging

Paige exits. Music ends. Lars gets out his mobile phone. He dials.

Lars (*into the phone*) Hi, I'd like to order some pizzas please. One vegetarian and a selection of others; five in total, ham and mushroom, yep, spicy chicken, something with spinach .

Hal Pepperoni

Lars And one with pepperoni. No seafood. The White Lodge, Oak Avenue. Tell the guy there's a big tip if he gets here quickly. Yes, I know it is; just tell him to get here

Lars puts his phone back in his jacket. Paige enters.
She sits.

Siân How long do you think it takes them to die?

Paige Until the last synapse stops firing? A minute or two

Siân A long time

Paige An eternity, I should think. Which just leaves you, my love. What kismet for your lobster?

Lars Waiter?

The Waiter enters.

Would you take that away?

Paige Are you asking him to cook it for you? How godlike

Lars I don't give a damn what he does with it. Take it away

The Waiter is about to remove the lobster.

Paige Don't touch it

Lars Take it away

Paige Don't touch it

Lars Waiter, would you please get rid of this?

Pause.

What fee have you offered him?

Paige Twenty-five thousand pounds

Lars Sure. I'll double whatever my wife has offered you, if you take this thing away. Let's make it a hundred quid

Pause.

Five hundred, cash

Mike I would definitely take that

Paige His motivation's far more complex than you think. He doesn't work for money alone. He has charitable principles

Lars He's doing this for charity?

Paige The biblical sense of it. The sense that's often translated as love

Lars I see
 (*to the Waiter*) One thousand pounds

Paige You can't bribe a man of integrity

Lars Very well, it can stay there. We can watch it slowly drown in air

Mike Not wanting to be crass or anything, Lars, but if I took it away would you give me a thousand pounds?

 Wynne takes Lars' lobster out to the patio.

Paige Waiter, we need drinks. Thank you so much

 The Waiter exits.

Lars So he calls it love?

Paige He calls it service. I call it love

Lars That's very sad

Paige There's nothing sad about love, my darling

 Wynne enters. She sits.

Lars (*to Wynne*) Thank you

Wynne That's OK . . . It's in the pond, but what about your goldfish?

Paige We're having them tomorrow, with pasta

Wynne And I thought Lars was exaggerating when he warned me about you

Lars (*to Paige*) I warn everyone

Paige is taken by surprise. She seems to crumble.

Mike Paige, can I ask you a rude and personal question?

Paige Yes

Mike What do you do, you know, for a living? While Lars is writing his books and that?

Paige Mike, how sweet of you to think that I might do something
  I do nothing. I never have

The Waiter enters with drinks. He serves them.

Hal Come on, Paige
  All that personal grooming. I wouldn't call that nothing
  And you organise things for charity

Lars Oh, call it love

Hal You're always making us buy those effing raffle tickets

Paige Flowers For The Homeless

Hal And there's your genius in the kitchen

Lars She's always visiting the penguin pond at the zoo

Hal And Paige, half the vintners in Kensington would go out of business if it weren't for you

Paige You see, Mike, my life is chock-full. And if ever I tire of these thrilling pursuits, there's always the Open University or psychotropic drugs

  The Waiter exits.

Mike It's just that I think you'd be very good at what I do

Paige You mean

Mike Yeh

Paige You think I'd make a good thief?

Mike Burglar, yeh

Paige (*moved*) Really?

Mike You've got the nerve, I can tell

Paige Mike, I'm thrilled

Lars Hah

Paige I'm unbelievably moved that you should think that

Mike I think you'd actually love it. Have you never considered crime as a career?

Paige Well, it wasn't one of the options at school and I hardly need the money, do I?

Mike You'd do it for the subversion

Paige Yes, yes

Mike It's such a thrill

Paige I'm sure

Mike And no one would suspect you in the way that they all instantly suspect me. As soon as I walked in here, you had me sussed, didn't you? Whereas you're –

Paige Such a posh bitch

Mike You could get in anywhere; pilfer anything. You could do top jobs

The Waiter enters with two cooked lobsters. He places one in front of Siân and one in front of Paige.

Paige Oh look
Yum yum

Siân Could I have some HP sauce, please?

Hal sighs loudly.

What?
Bring me some ketchup as well

The Waiter exits. Siân cracks her lobster open. She removes the intestines.

Hal What about me, Mike? What are my chances in the crime league? Because between you and me I'm effing sick of my job and I'd love a bit of stealth, bit of ducking and diving, dodging and weaving, breaking and entering, you know what I mean?

Mike Well, actually, Hal, don't take this the wrong way, but I wouldn't trust you

Hal Oh great

Mike Not that I think you'd try and / personally stab me in the back or anything

Hal No, no, no, that's great, Mike

Mike I just think you might lose your cool under pressure and, you know, do something stupid or violent

Hal Trigger-happy, you mean?

Mike Well –

Hal Effing great. Psycho Hal, loose with a sawn-off shotgun. Watch out, Twickenham, here I come

He aims and fires an imaginary machine gun at all the characters, letting off a long volley at Siân. She continues to devour her lobster. Hal runs out of steam.

Siân (*to Paige*) This is absolutely sensational

Wynne I once tried to shoplift some earrings from Laura Ashley – must be about fifteen years ago – and I was so tense that I almost had a nervous breakdown. I was sweating and shaking and I stuck them in my pocket and crept past the till having this awful panic attack – I could barely see; I was nearly sick – then I felt so guilty that I went back and paid for them and they were such a rip-off and they turned out to be horrible anyway and I cried

Lars Poor you

The Waiter enters with condiments. Siân liberally helps herself.

Mike You would definitely be the worst burglar that ever lived

Siân I'd like to be a con artist

Mike Good choice

Siân I'd like to disguise myself as someone warm and caring and rip off the old, the vulnerable and the bereaved

Mike Certainly a challenge

Siân Total moral corruption: tough one to crack

Lars And what about me, Mike?

Paige You are a con artist, my love

Lars You're so funny. You are so hilarious. Look; my sides have split

Mike Well, Lars, I'd actually put you right at the top of a huge crime ring. I'd say you wouldn't be so good on the ground but you've got the nous to hire a couple of heavies and a good accountant to do it all for you. You have the, um –

Paige Sang froid, the glacial, hyperborean stare

Mike The, er –

Hal The cool

Mike I just don't think anyone would fuck with you

Hal He's effing perceptive, this kid, isn't he? For a tea leaf

Mike Paige?

Paige Mike

Mike Could I use your toilet, please?

Paige Of course

Mike I've been busting for a while but I didn't like to say

Paige Mike, I want you to feel that our home is yours. (*to the Waiter*) Would you show our guest to the little boys' room?

Mike I'm not going to rip anything off; it's OK

Paige Oh, feel free. Take the Cupid; it's French, seventeenth century; ever so pricey. Lars gave it to me on our tenth anniversary. I use it as a loo-roll stand

Mike Are you sure?

Paige It would probably double as a very good kosh. You could keep it in your van for emergencies

Mike You think of everything

Paige The sign of a good hostess

> *The Waiter shows Mike out. Lars gets out his mobile phone. He dials.*

Siân Paige, I genuinely think this is the best dead thing I ever ate

Paige That's great

Siân And do you know what's particularly satisfying about it?

Paige You killed it yourself

Siân It's an honest meal

Lars Police, please

Paige (*leaping up*) Don't you dare. Don't you DARE!

Lars Hello, yes, I'd like to report a burglary

Paige grapples with Lars for the phone.

Paige He's a guest in your house

Lars He's a parasite

Paige You invited him in!

Lars To use a phone

Paige Well he's staying

Lars He's a two-bit thief

Paige And you're a ten-pound cunt

Wynne Uhh!

Lars (*struggling*) Get – off – you

Paige I will not have police in this house!

The guests watch in silence as the struggle becomes more vicious.

Lars GET – OFF!

Lars shoves Paige away from him.

Yes, hello, this is Lars Janssen at The White Lodge, Oak Avenue. I'd like to report a burglary. That's correct, yes

Paige knees Lars in the groin. He doubles up. She takes the phone.

Paige Hello, this is Paige Janssen, Oak Avenue
I'm so sorry, my husband should never have called you

Hal Holy batcrap

Lars (*to Hal*) Get / me the phone

Hal hesitates. The Waiter enters. Paige motions him to stay where he is.

Paige He's on medication – this is terribly painful to say –
for pre-senile dementia and he's having a persecution
episode

Hal (*holding his hand out for the phone*) Come on,
Paige. Be decent

Paige Well, he thinks there's a burglar in the house but
I'm afraid to say that the poor man he's picked on is
actually one of our dinner guests. No, it's a degenerative
psychosis; really sad . . . No, that absolutely won't be
necessary; I have his medication right here. Yes, yes.
Thank you. You're most understanding

Paige ends the call. She hands the phone to the Waiter.

Paige Would you throw that into the pond, please?

The Waiter exits. Paige sits. Lars sits.

Lars One day, Paige, you will get what you deserve

Paige Yes. I will

Hal That was really ugly, guys

*Wynne puts out her hand to Lars. Lars takes it. Paige
acknowledges this. Mike returns with a seventeenth-
century Cupid. There's a toilet roll on its arrow.*

Mike Is this the thing you meant?

Lars releases Wynne's hand.

Paige Do you like it?

Mike Yeh, it's really nasty

Paige It's yours

Mike Are you sure?

Paige Only if you promise to keep it in your toilet

Mike No fucking problem, Paige
Thanks very much

Lars I'm afraid it's not yours to give

Paige Do all the presents you've given me over the years still belong to you? What about Beaky?

Lars What?

Paige My penguin. Is he still yours?

The Waiter enters. Mike puts the toilet roll on the floor. He turns the Cupid upside down and swings it like a golf club, hitting the toilet roll. It leaves a trail of paper, coming to rest at Lars's feet. Mike sits, the Cupid beside him. Pause. Siân belches loudly.

Paige We need drinks

The Waiter exits.

Paige Do you know, I had a feeling that conversation might flag at this point in the evening; with everyone feeling so replete, so carried away on a tide of bonhomie, so in order to facilitate an easy flow of chat, I've arranged a little game. Under your side plates, everybody, I've put an envelope. In the envelope there's a card with something written on it. You simply have to read the card and then stand up and speak for two minutes on whatever it inspires you to say. Now, who's first?

Hal I hate games

Paige Then get the ball rolling

Hal No, thanks

Siân I will

Paige Splendid

Siân I like games

Siân stands and opens the envelope.

Mike Um, sorry, Paige, but my envelope says Bob

Paige Yes, Bob is Wynne's ex-lover, who couldn't attend – because his genitals are hanging in her gallery – but Mike, we're very fortunate to have you here in his place

The Waiter enters with drinks. He serves them.

Siân Murder Weapons. What makes you think I'm qualified to speak about this?

Paige I should think everyone's qualified

Siân Murder Weapons?

Paige Just speak. First thing that comes into your head

Siân You mean what would I use if I were going to murder someone?

Paige Just in fun, of course

Siân A lance. (*She mimes lancing Hal across the table.*)
A cudgel, a meat cleaver, a chainsaw, a saucepan over the head, the flex from a mobile-phone charger, um, a cluster bomb, a bin liner, rat poison, chloroform, an asp, a blunderbuss, a pump-action automatic shotgun –

Paige That's certainly a favourite of mine

Siân A pit filled with tigers

Mike A pool filled with sharks

Siân A malmsey butt

Mike What?

Siân It's a tub of sherry; you can drown in it. A mallet, any kind of electrical appliance and a bath

Mike Death by hairdryer

Siân Kalashnikovs, hand grenades, daggers, a flick knife, a penknife

Wynne Pliers

Siân Pliers?

Wynne I'm sure you could murder someone with pliers

Hal Really slowly

Mike Lead piping

Siân Yes, candlestick, revolver, hatpin, neutron bomb, boiling oil

Mike A scorpion

Siân Red-hot poker

Mike Any kind of poisonous frog or spider

Siân Blow dart

Wynne Tights

Mike Bow and arrow

Siân Tights?

   Wynne mimes being hanged with a pair of tights.

Mike Liquidiser

Siân How?

Mike If it was a giant one

Siân Right. Razor blade, javelin

Hal An anthrax spore

Siân A concrete mixer, plastic explosives, killer ants

Wynne Can't you kill someone with noise? You know. if it's subliminal enough it makes all your internal organs implode or something

Siân Noise, a peanut, a letter-opener, thin ice

Hal A ducking stool

Siân A sword, quicksand, mercury in the ear

Mike Wow

Siân A set of darts, bees

Mike Wasps

Wynne Cheese

Siân Pardon?

Wynne You could plug every orifice with cheese

Lars Cool

Siân A bull whip, a cruise missile, mustard gas, nerve gas

Mike Calor gas

Siân A truncheon, a baseball bat, a cat-o'-nine-tails, um mud

Mike One of those things with spikes coming out of it on the end of a chain

Siân Yes, a –

Mike What are they called?

Siân A gladiator thing

Mike One of those

Lars A flail

Siân A flail, thank you. A trident

Mike A trident missile

Siân A syringe full of air

Wynne A combine harvester

Siân OK

Hal Weaponised marburg

Wynne What's that?

Siân Oh, some microbe or other

Hal It's a filovirus. It chomps away at human body organs – including the skin – until they liquefy, so that victims die awash in their own blood and putrefaction

Siân Thank you, Hal. Weaponised marburg

Wynne Um, one of those things that crushes cars in scrapyards

Siân A hacksaw, an electricity pylon, a banana skin at the top of a cliff, a plastic bag

Mike Gaffer tape

Hal Botulism, ebola

Siân Any other fucking microbe, have we had bleach?

Wynne Don't think so

Siân Bleach, a silver bullet

Mike A voodoo curse

Siân (*she holds up a lobster knife*) And one of these.
That must be two minutes

Paige Jolly good

> *Paige starts a round of applause. Siân sits.*

Siân I had a lot of help

Paige You missed out my favourite

Lars A stake through the heart

Paige A traitor's kiss

Siân What about a lobster? Could you kill someone with
a lobster?

Paige Only if you poisoned it

Hal And have you?

Paige No

Hal Shame

Siân What did you say?

Hal Nothing

Siân What did you fucking say, Hal?

Hal I was making a joke

Siân Well, I'm on the floor

Paige When it comes down to it, if you really wanted to
kill someone it would have to be a knife, wouldn't it?
They're so readily available, so hard to trace
And silent
(*to the Waiter*) What do you think?
You don't have to answer that
Poor chap, I'm embarrassing him
Now, Hal, I'm sure you'd love to follow Siân

Hal No thanks

Paige Oh, don't be a spoilsport. Come on

Hal No

Mike Shall I open Bob's?

Paige Good idea, Mike. We need drinks

The Waiter exits. Mike stands and opens his envelope.

Mike And the winner is . . .
Telling The Truth
Oh

Paige Bob's a politician, you see. I thought truth'd stump him

Mike Two minutes on the truth?
Fuck
Why is it that lies seem much more definite than truth?
One person's vision of truth can be another's crock of
shite. Why is that? What do you think, Lars? Because
as a great thinker I suppose you deal with truth all the
time. Are we scared of it or are lies just better fun?

Lars I think you're shirking the issue, Mike

Mike And what issue is that?

Lars Telling The Truth

Mike You want the truth, Lars?

Lars I think we should be on the level, Mike

The Waiter enters with drinks. He serves them.

Mike OK. On the level: I'm a van driver, freelance. At
the moment I'm delivering for a company in King's Cross
that mass-produces cakes

Lars Cakes?

Mike Yes

Hal What, as in cakes?

Mike And trifles, yes

Hal You deliver cakes?

Mike Throughout the Greater London and Home Counties area. They offered me the Midlands too, but I said no

Hal So you're not a burglar?

Mike No

Hal So everything you've told us has been a lot of pork pies?

Mike I was in the army and I did witness the deaths of three people but, everything else – yes

Wynne Mike, you've told us lies

Mike Right the way down the line

Hal Effing typical

Wynne Why did you feel you had to lie to us?

Mike I didn't feel I had to. I just wanted to

Wynne Have we intimidated you somehow?

Mike No

Wynne Because I'm sure no one's meant to. Is it a class thing? Because, like I said, I'm very nearly the same class as you. And I'm Welsh

Lars He's lied because he's a nobody who does a shit-boring job

Mike That must be it

76

Wynne Oh Mike, did you think it would make you seem more interesting?

Mike Paige, I still think that if you ever decided to opt for a life of crime that you'd be fantastic at it and that if you ever need a driver or any kind of a sidekick, I'm your man

Paige Thank you

Mike Because just from lying about it I think I'm beginning to develop a bit of an aspirational fantasy in that direction

Paige Are you?

Mike Do aspirational fantasies generally start out as lies, Lars? Because just to come back to telling the truth for a minute – now that we're on the level – I'd like to ask you something

Lars Fire away

Mike Do you believe everything it says in your book?

Lars Absolutely

Mike Do you live by it?

Lars Of course

Mike You think you're the god of your own psyche-drive?

Lars Who isn't, Mike?

Mike And you can control your own destiny and everything just by wanting it to happen?

Lars I follow the primary life-force instinct

Mike Sorry, which is?

Wynne The instinct of I Want

Mike OK. So don't you think you might be living a lie?

Lars Why would I think that?

Wynne Mike, you haven't even read it yet

Mike You're right. So help me with something: supposing it was my aspirational fantasy to come here and join your party tonight? As a nobody with a shit-boring job, suppose I thought I could change my life by eating with you kind and shining people here? That if I was to sit with you at your table, I'd somehow leave a different man? What would your book tell me to do?

Lars It would tell you to be audacious

Mike Right

Lars It would tell you to do or die

Mike Do or die; right. And supposing, once I'd achieved my fantasy – been accepted at your table and treated like your home was mine – supposing I found that the shining people were actually hollow and lost and alone? Suppose I found that for all their glittering ideas they were twice as empty and miserable as me? You see, what if my aspirational fantasy turned out to be shit in my hands? What would your book tell me then?

   Pause.

Siân It would say – and put me right if I'm wrong here, Lars – it would say you've actually achieved it. When your fantasy loses it, allure you move on

Mike What to?

Siân The next step. The next aspiration

Mike So I'd just be chasing a bigger rainbow?

Siân I think the expression Lars uses is 'the Consumption of Experience'

Mike I'd be consuming experience?

Siân Yeh

Mike Like food?

Siân I think so

Mike But there's always a waste product with food, isn't there? I mean whether you've consumed lobster or a curry or whatever. What's the waste product with experience? I mean what do you do with it?

Wynne Listen, Mike
It's through experience you find enlightenment and I don't think there's anything hollow or empty about that

Mike I just want to know what you do with your shit

Wynne *Beyond Belief* is the most life-enhancing book I've ever read.
OK?

Mike I think my two minutes are up, Paige

Mike sits.

Paige Bravo, Mike

Mike Can I still keep this Cupid even though I've lied?

Paige Of course; it's for your loo

Mike Thank you

Paige You have got a loo, haven't you?

Mike I didn't lie about that

Paige I'm so glad. So that's one fact we know for sure; you're a man with a flush. And I think that answers your question about what to do with your metaphorical waste. Pull the chain and forget it existed. Isn't that right, Lars? Although I'm sure you put it far more eloquently in your book. Now, Hal, stop brooding and open your envelope

Hal No

Paige Why not?

Hal I don't like your game

Paige (*to Siân*) He's a terrible sulker, isn't he? Go on. It's all in the name of fun

Hal I bet

Paige And I'm dying to hear your remarks. You'll have so much to say

Hal stands and opens his envelope.

Hal I have nothing to say. Nothing to say on this subject at all

Hal screws up his card and throws it onto the floor. He sits.

Paige Oh Hal, come on. Be a player

Lars What did you give him?

Paige I think it was The Euro. Don't know why he's so upset

Hal It was Suicide Attempts

Lars That's beneath even you

Hal I have not one word to say

Lars You calculating bitch

Paige It was Suicide actually. A suicide *attempt* is a failure to achieve it

Hal Well, why don't you talk about it, Paige, seeing as you're the effing expert?

Paige I gave you the subject because you're the expert, Hal. How many times did Mags / attempt suicide?

Hal You gave me the subject because you hate me with a vengeance because you once drunkenly tried to shag me / and I said no

Paige You liar! I was crying on your shoulder / and you took advantage

Hal With your vodka-soaked tongue down my throat?

Paige You conceited PIG

Hal That's the kind of friend / you were to Mags

Paige Oh, the vanity!

Hal I had to peel you off, bat you away / like an effing *parasite*

Paige Do you honestly think I would touch you? I *know* you. Yuck

Hal The 'Yuck' is entirely mutual

Paige I'm with the Ancient Greeks and the Japanese on the subject of suicide

Lars Shut up

Paige I think it's a noble and honourable way to die

Lars I've had enough

Paige To take control of one's death requires the kind of courage that few of us possess. To attempt and fail is a tragedy. One has to seek and embrace it with complete dedication

Lars WELL WHY DON'T YOU?

Pause. Paige is crumbling.

81

Siân It was five times, actually. Once in her teens, once when she lost her baby, once when she heard about me, once when she was diagnosed with cancer and once more on our wedding day. Poor old Mags. Bit of a hobby really (*a hysterical giggle*)

Hal Jesus
You have no idea, no idea what you're talking about

Siân Oh, forgive me. Have I dared to speak of the precious Mags? I'm not worthy to mention her beloved name

Hal Until this moment I thought that Paige was the biggest bitch I'd ever met, but she's like a yappy lapdog next to you
You wait until the wound is open, then pounce
Like a slavering hyena

Siân D'you know something, Hal
You want to watch it

Hal Most contemptible beast in all the field

Siân You want to watch it

Hal Oh / do I?

Siân Because you're rapidly turning into one of the undead

Hal The what?

Siân Sucking youth and life out of the living
Like a dried-up, burnt-out, stuck-on barnacle

Hal And you
Are a praying mantis looking for a mate! /
You want to fuck me

Siân Oh, stop this disgusting self-pity / and get on with your life

Hal Then pull my head off and devour it
  Just like you did to that lobster

Siân I didn't fuck the lobster
  You Stupid Sad Old Man

  Pause. Siân is determined not to cry.

Wynne Um, shall we, you know, talk about something
else? We're all getting a bit bogged down in
  You know
  Grimness
  And, um

Hal Siân

Siân What?

Hal I am not undead

Siân And I am not a
  I'm your wife, you lucky cunt

Wynne Look, I'm sorry, but please
  Cunt is an orchid, a moist purse
  It's the apex of eroticism, not an expletive

Hal Why do you undermine me in front of my friends?

Siân Because you don't shape up, Hal. You do not
fucking shape up

Hal Then why, why did you throw yourself at me?

Siân You / FOOL

Hal I'm your husband

Siân No

Hal You lucky purse

Siân No!

Hal What d'you mean, no? I effing married you, didn't I?

Siân No, I don't know *who* you are! I don't even know what *job* you do

Who the *fuck* are you, Hal?

Hal I've told you about my

Siân exits.

Shit

Hal follows her out.

Paige We need drinks

The Waiter exits.

Wynne I know Siân's probably a post-feminist and everything and she thinks that in trying to reinvent the word cunt she's empowering herself – or something – but I don't think it gives her an excuse. She's abusing a beautiful thing

Mike Why don't you open your envelope, Wynne?

Paige Great idea

Wynne (*to Lars*) Shall I?

Lars (*standing*) I'll open it

Lars takes Wynne's envelope and opens it.

Lars (*he reads*) How Wynne met Lars. Do you know, it would be a pleasure to speak about this

Wynne Oh, yes, go on please. It's a funny story. Let's have a funny story

Paige Ha

Lars This is more than twenty years ago, long before I

When we were

Wynne Gorgeously young

Lars Wynne came to my stall at the Freshers' Fair. She was in the first year and I was in the third, sole member of the Nietzsche For Now Soc. She was such a breath of fresh air. She was wearing this green skirt – a terrible thing, which it later transpired she'd made herself

Wynne Out of that pretend turf you get in greengrocers. I thought it was so Bowie

Lars Anyway, she asked who Nietzsche was and I tried to tell her about Zarathustra and the Will To Power and she made a joke

Wynne I said willy to power because it sounded like a lot of cock

Lars You remember

Wynne Yes

Lars And she smiled and these dimples came into her cheeks – look, still there – and my knees went completely weak. Anyway she went and joined the Wooden Earrings Society or something and I felt bereft. She wasn't interested

The Waiter enters with drinks. He serves them.

Wynne I was a feminist separatist then and I thought I was a lesbian but it was just a phase and anyway I was still a virgin so what did I know – although I still find women attractive

Lars Great. Anyway I found out she was studying Art with Drama so I started to hang out with the Artniks. When I heard she was in a production of *The House of Bernarda Alba* I put myself forward for one of the roles and got laughed out of the room

Wynne I was playing that girl whose breasts burst like pomegranates and that's when I began to think about eroticism as a means of personal growth. Of course I was reading a lot of Anaïs Nin at the time

85

Lars She'd died her hair black. Why?

Wynne And I started to look for a man who could, you know, take my cherry. It was becoming such a burden. I mean, I'd slept with women but I just thought I wouldn't know myself until I'd had that penile experience. Nin spoke about being joyously impaled on a man's sensual mast and I thought crikey, that sounds fun. And there was Lars, hanging around with books of German philosophers under his arm and a badge saying 'Vote for the Antichrist'

Lars Wynne I had no idea it was your cherry

Wynne Oh, you must have known

Lars I hadn't a clue. I feel really honoured

Wynne I was just using you as a sex object

Lars Well, anytime

Wynne giggles. Siân enters followed by Hal. He is trying to embrace her.

Hal I am trying to live. What do you think I'm trying to do?
Do you think it's easy?

Siân returns his embrace with a sob.

Siân No I don't
I don't
I don't

They hold each other.

Wynne Why don't I open your envelope?

Lars Don't bother; it's / a stupid game

Wynne I want to. I really do

Hal I'm so sorry. My poor baby

Siân (*pushing him away*) Oh God
  I am not your fucking

Hal Siân, please

Siân Why do I –
  Why do I (*love you*)

  Siân exits. Hal follows. Wynne opens Lars' envelope.

Wynne Death

Lars Oh, don't touch it

Wynne I want to

Lars Don't even go near it

Wynne I can and I will. Willy to power

Paige We need drinks

Lars We've got fucking drinks, my love

  The Waiter exits. Wynne prepares herself.

Wynne Death is the end of life
  If I was to paint it, it would be hideous and yet
  I don't think death is a hideous thing
  It is physically hideous and that makes us afraid
  But as I said earlier I've actually come to a calm place
about death
  A place of resigned –

Paige Inspired resignation was the wonderful phrase

Wynne Yes. I don't know whether I should say
  But yes
  My mother died a year ago and
  And actually one of the things that helped me move
away from that place was Lars' book
  As he says
  Nothing enhances life more than death

87

The Waiter enters with drinks. He serves them.

Knowing that we face death,
  We are forced to live
  Or succumb to darkness
  Um, I used to think that –
  I can only say it in the words of Keats –
  'It would be sweet to die, to cease upon the midnight
with no pain'
  That to hurl oneself at death would be somehow to
cheat it
  That death was linked to desire
  That if death was a figure he would be Byronic in
a dark suit
  Death would wear Hugo Boss
  But now I think that death is nothing
  And that nothing is everything
  I can face it calmly and feel its power
  It must be the biggest orgasm one ever has
  That's all. The end

Lars Nothing is everything. Everything is nothing.
You're right

Wynne Bit waffly

Lars Well done

Lars holds up his glass. Wynne clinks it with hers.

Wynne Aren't you going to eat your lobster, Paige?
Having gone to the trouble of murdering it

Paige I'm going to have it preserved and made into a
telephone

Siân enters.

Siân Just chucked up

Wynne Oh no

Siân Really barfed

Wynne Where?

Siân looks round as Hal enters. He's taken his jacket and shirt off. He wears a white vest and Lars' trousers from the opening scene.

Hal Um got a bit hot
Saw these down by the pool
Thought I'd try 'em for size

Lars They look cool, Hal
Really cool

Paige Waiter, could you clear? I think we've finished with the main

The Waiter begins to clear.

Siân Hal

Hal (*angrily*) What?

Siân Nothing

Lars Don't you have an envelope, my love?

Paige I thought it unfair to choose my own subject
So you have an envelope for me

Lars Do I?

Paige It arrived from your lawyer aeons ago and you put it in your desk
Why don't you go and fetch it?

Lars Whatever you wish, my love

Lars exits.

Siân Mike, while you were on the loo getting your Cupid, Lars tried to call the police to tell them that you'd robbed next door. Paige grabbed the phone and stopped him. Just thought you might like to know

Mike Thanks. Fuck

Wynne I don't think he wanted to shop you, Mike. I just think he wanted the police to know that, you know, there may have been a burglary next door and everything because, you know, they like to know these things

Mike Right. And Paige stood up for me?

Wynne Well, anyway, it doesn't matter because you just deliver cakes and it would have been awfully embarrassing if the police had come and searched your van and just found profiteroles

Siân (*to Hal*) I'm / pregnant

  Hal is dumbfounded.

Wynne I mean, you'd have looked silly and they'd have / been cross and

Mike I think it's time I went

Paige No

Mike I better had

Paige Don't go
  Please

  Lars returns with an envelope. He hands it to Paige. She opens it. She takes out some documents and reads.

How Lars Dumped Paige
  I'm sorry; it's just too boring
  So my subject for tonight
  Is T. E. Lawrence

Lars God spare us

Paige Yes
  One Christmas

My uncle who worked in the city threw a fabulous
party
    We were all to arrive in fancy dress
    And there was champagne and magic and dancing till
dawn
    I wanted to come as a gorilla but my mother forced
me into a
    Grecian robe

Lars Athene, goddess of order and justice

Paige I'd put rubber pythons in my hair
    And when I was announced
    Raging at the shallow splendour of it all
    The first thing I saw was a
    Dazzling young man
    Dressed as T. E. Lawrence
    He was just a graduate serving drinks
    But Uncle Moneybags liked him
    Liked the gleam of that pristine psyche-drive
    So he introduced me
    Lars of Arabia
    We ended up
    We laughed at them
    Laughed at their age and their lies
    And then in the darkness we

   Paige abruptly sits.

Etcetera

Hal (*to Siân*) Are you?

Siân Yes

   Hal starts to sob. He clings to Siân.

Wynne What is it? Have I missed something?

Paige (*leafing through the papers*) I think she's up the
spout

Wynne Oh gosh. That's super

Lars Well done, mate. Thrilled

Hal continues to sob. Siân is crying too.

Mike Have you got children, Paige?

Paige No

Mike I've got a daughter

Paige Oh?

Mike She's beautiful

Paige I don't doubt it

Mike Here

*He shows Paige a photograph. She discards the papers
and looks at it. She is moved.*

Mike She lives with her mum but I see her a lot

Paige She's very like you

Wynne I've got two grown-up sons
Tower over me
Can hardly believe it sometimes

Paige Thank you

Paige hands the photograph back to Mike.

Wynne One's doing GCSEs and the other's –
Well he's in rehab, actually

Lars (*sympathetically*) Hey

Paige They're wonderful, aren't they?
Offspring
You can lose yourself in their laughter and simplicity
And in their joy and openness you can forget
For years and years
That life is completely

Pause.

Mike Can I get you anything, Paige?

Paige Where's the waiter?

Waiter I'm here

Paige Yes

Paige takes the Waiter's hand.

Let's do as we arranged

The Waiter bows. He exits.

Lars And what's that, Paige? What have you arranged?

Paige Desserts
Just desserts

Scene Four

DESSERT

Hal and Siân are sitting together, the sobbing over. The Waiter is serving the diners with fancy frozen desserts. He finishes.

Paige (*to the Waiter*) We need drinks

Lars Yes, drinks, I'll have five

Paige Thank you

   The Waiter exits.

It seems that this is our last supper, darling
   And the dessert I've created is more appropriate than I hoped. It's an indication of what your life will be like without me

Hal What is it?

Paige Frozen Waste
   Tuck in

   Paige begins to eat. Mike joins her.

Mike This looks like a baked bean

Paige Probably is. I just went through the contents of yesterday's bin and added sugar

Mike Right. It's really tasty

Paige It contains no slaughterhouse products

Mike I think that's a cat treat

Paige And someone very lucky's got the furred tomato that I found at the back of the fridge

The Waiter enters with drinks. He serves them, giving five to Lars.

Mike Well, it's great, Paige. Really nice

Paige Thank you

Mike Is there any more?

Paige I'm afraid not. But I could always rustle some up. Our bin's a cornucopia of excess

Siân involuntarily retches. Paige and Mike continue to eat.

Hal What happened to those pizzas, Lars? Got a woman eating for two here

Lars Shall I phone and bother them?

Hal Expect the delivery kid's got lost in the fog. They send them out on those rickety little scooters; poor sod's probably come a cropper

Wynne My eldest son delivered pizzas for a while. I couldn't believe the conditions; I told him he should start a union. But he didn't seem to mind. Scooted about every night, happy as Larry. Turned out he was using it as a cover for his dealing

Paige What pizzas are we talking about?

Lars The pizzas I ordered when it became obvious that your food was inedible

Paige Has my meal failed to please you, my dearest love?

Lars No, I'm just thrilled with everything that you've done tonight

Paige Thank you for saying so. I tried so hard

Lars Your meal confirms everything that I believe about you

Paige I thought you'd gone Beyond Belief, Lars

Lars You're a black hole

Paige Really, dear?

Lars A centre of negativity, actively destructive of all that's around you

Paige That's nice

Lars The kindest thing I could say is that you're not responsible for the depth of your psychosis

Paige Thank you

Lars But I'm not kind, I'm truthful. You're a slow poison. And here in my house, surrounded by my friends I'm going to liberate myself. I wash my hands of you, Paige. You can creep to decrepitude alone

Paige Well
      That brings me on to my joke for the evening
      I think every hostess should have a joke up her sleeve. When her guests have drunken, sobbed and letched their way through her repast there's nothing quite like a funny joke to finish things off. It fills the air with joy and melts even the sternest of hearts. So. There once was a woman who –

Paige lets out an uncontrollable sob. It frightens her. She struggles to control herself.

Mike I think I know this joke
      There was once a woman who married a block of ice, thinking that it was a man

Lars What's the punch line, Mike?

Mike There isn't one. It's just a fucking joke

Lars I don't see anybody laughing

Mike Are you going to eat your Frozen Waste, Lars?

Lars No

Mike I think you ought

Lars Why?

Mike Because the dish was created in your honour

Lars I'm not hungry, Mike. Why don't you have it?

Mike Paige made it for you

Lars She hardly killed herself over it, did she? It's out of
the bin

Mike That's not the point

Lars I don't want it, thank you

Mike Why not?

Lars Because the thought of it makes me want to spew

Mike Lars, I think you should eat up your Frozen Waste

Lars I'm sorry?

Mike You should eat your Frozen Waste before it melts

Lars Mike, are you fucking with me? Why are you
trying to fuck with me at my own table? I don't think it's
very polite

Wynne Mike? Why have you taken a dislike to Lars?
    Only I think he's been nice to you
    He let you in here
    And I don't think he deserves it

Mike Do you know what I think, Wynne?

Wynne What?

Mike I think Lars is a cunt

   Pause.

Hal Well done, Paige. Must be nice to know you haven't lost your touch

Lars Yes, she's still got it, hasn't she?

Hal Good old Paige; it's quite amazing. She could always pull at thirty paces

Lars And so subtly too

Hal She has them wrapped round her finger before they're even aware. Mike, old pal; you're being had

Mike I'm not old, Hal. And I'm not your pal. I think you're a sad fuckwit

Hal I'm not sad

Mike And Lars is a cunt

Hal Listen, mate, you're a cocky little git and if you try anything funny I'm on your effing case

Mike What sort of funny thing do you think I might try? Ventriloquism?

Hal I'm warning you

Mike Well, I'm shitting myself

Hal You should be. I used to box for effing Wiltshire

Mike Is that some kind of a speech impediment you've got, that you can't say fucking?

Hal Watch it, tosser, or I'll punch your bollocks out through your throat

Siân Hal

Hal What?

Siân I beg you to grow up

Lars Why do you think I'm a cunt, Mike? I'm intrigued

Mike Well, frankly, Lars, you've got it tattooed on your forehead in big black letters

Hal Bullshit. You don't like Lars because he's got more money than you'll ever dream of and it's so obvious it's almost sad

Mike Why are you so loyal to him?
  He couldn't give a toss whether you lived or died

Wynne That's so not true

Mike He couldn't give a toss whether *anyone* lived or died

Wynne You're so wrong, Mike. Lars has a huge soul

Mike Wynne, good luck
  'Cause if you're throwing yourself at him you're going to need it
  That man is Frozen Waste
  He is totally fucking sterile
  There's about as much passion in him as there is in a dead penguin

Lars (*stands*) OK
  Party over, Mike

Mike Are you asking me to leave?

Lars I'm telling you. Get out

Paige Before we've had the cheeseboard? Unthinkable

Mike Um, Paige would like me to stay

Lars (*taking hold of Mike*) Out

Mike Ooops

Lars Get out

Mike Looks like I'm going, then

Lars Damn right

Lars frogmarches Mike to the exit. The Waiter is in front of it.

Mike Thanks for a really great dinner, Paige

Lars OUT

Paige (*to the Waiter*) He'll stay for coffee, of course

Lars SCUM

Mike (*handing Lars his book*) I think this is yours

Lars takes the book and flings it to the ground.

Lars Fuck off!

Mike I need my coat actually. He took my coat and I'm not leaving without it

Lars (*to the Waiter*) Get him his coat

Mike And my Cupid. Paige gave that to me and I'm taking it home to my bog

Lars I said get this scum his coat
Are you deaf?

Mike I mean seriously, pal, maybe you should get me my coat 'cause I can feel a big negative influxion coming your way

Lars Right
Move

Paige Are we ready for coffee, everyone?

Lars (*to the Waiter*) I SAID MOVE

Mike Perhaps he's waiting for you to say please

Lars GET OUT OF MY WAY

> *Lars flings Mike at the Waiter.*

Mike Sorry, excuse me

Paige Waiter
I think it's time

> *As the Waiter puts Mike neatly aside, he pulls out
> a knife, the movement almost invisible. He is staring
> at Lars, the threat of violence palpable. Silence.*

Paige Now then
Siân

Siân Yes?

Paige Would you like a coffee?

Siân Don't think so, no

Paige Coffee, Hal?

Hal What?

Paige I said would you like a coffee?

Hal What?

Paige How about you, Lars? Coffee?

Lars He's holding a knife

Paige Yes

Lars Why's that, Paige?

Paige It's all part of the service

Lars (*to the Waiter*) You; speak; why?

Paige Wynne, you'll have a coffee, won't you?

Wynne No

Paige Mike?

Mike I don't think so

Paige I also have herbal teas for anyone who's keen

Lars Who the hell are you?

Wynne You can deflect this, Lars
  Whatever it is
  Just refuse wound entry

Lars WHAT DO YOU WANT?

Paige Well, seeing as everyone's passed on coffee, I'll move straight on to my joke. There was once a woman who heard that you could get anything you desired on the / internet

Lars Shut up

Paige As she had a lot of time and money at her disposal she thought she'd see if this / was true

Lars You'd better tell me what's going on

Paige She thought, 'What is the thing I want most in all the world and / can't obtain?'

Lars What the FUCK

Paige After some time the answer came / to her

Lars Is going on?

Paige The woman wanted a person's death
  So she set about looking for a man who'd provide it

Lars You

Paige Days went by as she sat by her screen

Lars Are

Paige And just as she was on the point of giving up, she found what she was looking for: easefuldeath.com. The man used metaphors to describe what he could provide

but to those truly seeking an executioner his meaning
was clear

Lars Hal

Hal Yes

Paige He could provide death in a multitude of guises
and bring it right into your home. Highly exclusive

Lars Do something

Hal What?

Paige Now, there was only one person the woman knew
who truly deserved such a top-drawer death

Lars Just fucking

Hal Yes

Hal exits.

Paige This person yearned for peace, for freedom, for
passion. And what greater passion do we ever face than
the orgasm of our own mortality?

Lars So this is your man of integrity?

Paige Yes

Lars I don't believe you, not for a second

Paige Then you are true to your philosophy

Lars (*to Mike*) You; army man; what do we do?

Mike I don't know

Lars Think of something

Mike You could beg

Lars Intervene

Mike What, throw myself at a knife?

Lars For God's sake!

Mike Suppose it was an aspirational fantasy of mine
  To watch a cunt like you shit himself?

Lars (*to Paige*) All right, we've had a laugh. Game over

Paige Lars, we all have our moments of deadly earnest
  And this is one of mine

Lars How much have you paid him?

Paige I told you, twenty-five thousand pounds

Lars Cheap

Paige He's a charitable man

Lars You've got no idea
  No idea what you're doing

Paige Oh, give me credit

Lars (*to the Waiter*) Put the weapon down
  Put it down, keep the money and go

  Hal enters.

Hal Can't get your phone to work

Paige I disconnected them

Hal Where's your mobile?

Siân In the pond

Hal I need a phone, Lars

Wynne There's one in my coat

Hal Where's your coat?

Wynne (*pointing to the Waiter*) He took it
  Oh my God, oh my God

Hal Fucking fuck

  Hal exits.

Lars (*to the Waiter*) I'll double it
Fifty thousand, a hundred
What do you *want*?

Paige Oh Lars, don't disappoint me
I was hoping for inspiration – because what does one
say at the moment of one's death?
I've been trying to imagine it for weeks
One could try and lamely wheedle out of it
I suppose one could scream and run or stand and sing –
Bassey-style
Ending all on a piercing shrill
Or one could embrace the silence that's to come
Cleave the dark
And say nothing

*Paige has her arms around the Waiter so that the
knife is pointing at her heart. He stabs her.*
He helps her to the ground.

Waiter Shhhh . . . shhhh . . .

*As Paige dies, he puts his hand on her forehead with
the compassion and authority of a priest.*
He closes her eyes.
Lars drops to his knees.
Siân is shivering.
*The Waiter stands. He pulls a handkerchief from
his pocket and wipes the knife. He places it neatly
on the table.*
Mike lunges for him. The Waiter raises a hand.
Mike stops in his tracks.
*The Waiter removes the envelope of money from
his pocket.*

Lars Who are you?

*The Waiter takes two banknotes from the top of the
pile.*

Waiter My service is free
  I take only the wage of a waiter

  The Waiter places the rest of the money on the table.
  He bows. He leaves.
    A beat. Mike chases after him.

Siân Cold
  Want Hal

  Siân exits.
    Lars is staring at the body. Wynne approaches him.

Wynne Lars

  She touches him. Lars spins round.

Lars What are you –

Wynne I was –

Lars What do you want?

Wynne Trying to

  Lars is looking at her as if she is a stranger. Wynne
  falters. Lars turns back to Paige.

Lars, what can I do?
  There must be something I can do
  Some action to
  Tell me, what can I do?

Lars Nothing

  Hal and Siân enter.

Hal There's no
  No signal
  We couldn't
  No one's coming
  The fog seems to be
  I mean
  In the house

Siân Freezing

Mike enters.

Mike I couldn't find him
He just vanished
It was like
No sound, nothing

The lights flicker. They go out.

Couldn't find my way back in
Floundering
Thick white dark

Wynne Why has the light gone out?
Who's done this?
Where's the light?

Siân Cold

Wynne Give us the light back
Give us light

Breathing. A palpable sense of fear.

Lars Nothing